GIA GANESH

CAREER INC:

THE BUSINESS OF YOU

Copyright Information

DEDICATION

This book is dedicated to all career-minded profession-als looking to make strides in their career!

CRUSH YOUR CAREER GOALS!

CONTENTS

INTRODUCTION

"It is in your moments of decision that your destiny is shaped."
~Tony Robbins~

Most people would never, ever think of jumping out of a moving train. After all, such a move is scary, dangerous, and *definitely* crazy.

I guess I'm not like most people, though. I jumped.

Back in my early 20's, I got on the train to the wrong city and I panicked. As the train started moving, I asked a fellow passenger where the train was headed and realized I was going to the wrong place. Utter panic clouded my judgment, and I did what I thought was my only choice - I threw my luggage on to the platform and jumped. Unlike trains in the US, trains in India have unlocked doors, making the choice that much easier for me. Luckily for me, I walked away relatively unscathed from my daredevil stunt (except for a herniated disc in my neck – *ouch*).

How many times have *you* been in similar situations in your career or job?

One day you're chugging along on the slow-moving train of your current career when you realize that you're headed in the wrong direction, to the wrong destination. Soon, you're looking for ways to jump: jump without a plan; jump without considering the implications, you just want to jump. On the other hand, some people fail to jump even when it's desperately needed. For instance, maybe you continue traveling to the wrong destination rather than taking a much-needed **bold** step, because it feels safer. You believe that you have no other choice, and fail to see the different possibilities that may exist by choosing the first (and often painful) option. You're blinded by the panic and frustration of your situation, which intensifies when you remember that you don't have a backup plan. You don't have anyone to ask for trusted advice, which emphasizes how helpless and alone you feel. Fear keeps you paralyzed and stuck in the same spot.

Now, consider the alternative.

Imagine having a perfect career - a career where all elements work smoothly together, like the internal gears of a clock. Each gear plays an important role by working with the other gears in an intrinsic process to create the end result: the display of the right time.

In the perfect career world, all the gears would move smoothly and in sync to produce a fulfilling job that is financially rewarding with opportunities for growth and recognition.

Isn't it the right time for you to find *your* perfect career?

It may be hard to even imagine this, but try. Take a leap of faith and try to visualize how it would feel to live your perfect career every day.

You may have experienced bits and pieces of the perfect career from time to time. A word of appreciation, a bonus or a promotion, or a day working on an exciting and challenging project are a few examples you may have encountered.

"Why can't every single day be an embodiment of my perfect career?" you think, frustrated. But sadly, it disappears after raising your hopes and giving a glimpse of what could be.

For most people, it remains a figment of their imagination and never comes to fruition.

Instead, you experience frustration, pain, burnout, stagnation or boredom on a daily basis. The impact of these negative emotions spills over to all aspects of your life.

Warren Buffet famously said,

"There comes a time when you ought to start doing what you want. Take a job that you love. You will jump out of bed in the morning. I think you are out

of your mind if you keep taking jobs that you don't like because you think it will look good on your resume. Isn't that a little like saving up sex for your old age?"

I am here to tell you that it is POSSIBLE to achieve this sense of fulfillment with a financially rewarding and growth-inducing career. How? By applying yourself to the *Business of You*.

◆ ◆ ◆

REWIND

First, let me take you back in time and give you some context around how and why this book came to be.

I grew up in a traditional and conservative middle-class family in Bangalore, India. My dad worked as a mechanical engineer for the same boss for over 35 years. My dad's commitment to one boss is unlike what most people can or will experience in today's workplace. Eventually, he retired and guess what he did then? He went to work as a consultant for that same boss he'd had for so many years! As of the time of writing this book, this is still the case.

Can you imagine working for the same boss for your *entire life*? Would that be an element of your perfect career?

My mother took a different route. Despite receiving her Master's Degree in Science, she chose to be a homemaker and care for my brother and me.My parents were my role models then.

So, why did my parents choose this particular path?

My parents always emphasized the importance of a good school and a good education for us. They sacrificed other things in order to ensure we received a good education that would pave the path for a good future. Our priority was always education so we could get a good job. I was always aware of that and did pretty well in school and carried it over into college. Once I entered the IT work world, I was just another average joe; here were many other 'freshers' (as we were called) who had procured jobs through campus placements in the IT/tech industry. We were driven then purely by our pay package and working for a multinational corporation (MNC). MNC's were known to provide opportunities to work abroad.

I did what everyone did. I got paid like everyone too. And I felt the same as others – "Will this job take me abroad? And how do I climb the rungs of the corporate ladder?"

In the early 2000's, supervisors did not provide guidance to help employees climb up the ladder. We did the work of writing and testing software programs for US clients such as Citibank, Michelin Tires, and Blue Cross Blue Shield, to name a few. There was no plan in place to help us develop as professionals, and I felt lost at times. I felt like I was capable of more, but did not know how to figure it out. I resigned myself to doing what everyone else was doing - a.k.a. follow the crowd. But the spark of doubt about my latent capabilities and potential and hope to do more still kept burning strong.

However, it was not until my early twenties when I started working and was seeking my Master's that things started coming together for me. It wasn't instantaneous, but was noticeable, like a lightbulb that flickers for a little bit when the light switch is turned on - eventually it strengthens and shines brightly.

I began to realize that I could shape my career destiny. I can pave a path for my career growth and advancement. I have more to offer than what is listed on my resume or LinkedIn profile. And the fledgling concept of the *Business of You* started growing in my head.

I progressed through my career and started gathering nuggets of wisdom from other professionals. As part of the leadership development efforts for the management-consulting firm I worked in, I started interacting and working closely with C-level executives. High potential identification and advancement projects with these C-level executives led to further insights on what truly distinguishes successful professionals. The insights I garnered solidified the *Business of You* framework in my head. I started applying it to my own career and began to see doors open that would never have opened for me before!

Truly, there is no better way to describe my professional journey in life thus far. There have been moments of glory and moments of darkness, moments of insights mingled with following the crowd. During the moments of darkness when I did choose to follow the crowd, I did not have one important thing—a mentor to guide me. I stumbled around in the dark trying to find and figure out the ropes.

I always desired to advance and progress by leaps and bounds. I wanted to make waves at the places I worked for, but I had one problem: there was no one to guide me or help me focus on the specific things to do and the steps to take. And, *that* is where this book comes in. This book is a gift to people like my younger self, filled with insights that I wish I'd known then. It's a gift to anyone who is looking to make the most out of their professional journey in life.

My aspirations with this book are to enlighten everyone, whether you're twenty, thirty, or older about what you can do to create a better career for yourself and manage it by using a different perspective!

To achieve this, we must first learn to OWN our careers, not hand over the reins of our career to our supervisors, the organizations that we work for, or the economy at large. Then it's time to make a shift towards a well rounded, intentional, and holistic approach to your career development.

◆ ◆ ◆

KNOWING YOUR NEEDS

One of my personal heroes and greatest sources of inspiration is Tony Robbins. He's a world-famous motivational speaker and performance expert. What compels me most about his expertise is how his speeches, as well as the information he shares, are both uplifting and thought-provoking.

An important concept that Mr. Robbins talks about is our six human needs that we all experience, which are[1]:

1. **Certainty**: assurance you can avoid pain and gain pleasure
2. **Uncertainty/variety**: the need for the unknown, change, new stimuli
3. **Significance**: feeling unique, important, special or needed
4. **Connection/love**: a strong feeling of closeness or union with someone or something
5. **Growth**: an expansion of capacity, capability, or understanding
6. **Contribution**: a sense of service and focus on helping, giving to, and supporting others

These needs serve as the basis for every decision and action we take both personally and professionally, impacting the quality of our lives. You may be surprised to read this, but our careers are an ideal platform to help us experience all of these needs!

I connect people with careers that meet these needs so they can learn to take a holistic approach to their success.

In our professional lives:

- Our desire to feel **certainty** is met by having the same place of work to go to every day. This place offers us a certain amount of financial security and comfort.

  - Our desire for different challenges at work, or even

moving into a different line of work, helps to satisfy our need for **uncertainty/variety**.

- Our desire to feel wanted for our skills and abilities caters to our need for **significance**.

- Our core need of craving a **connection** and acceptance is met through our interactions with colleagues and the friendships we cultivate at work.

- Our need to **grow** intellectually and emotionally is met through opportunities to take on new roles and advance our career. The further we advance in our careers, the more we grow emotionally. This is a natural progression because the higher you go; the more your career is likely to focus on people management, which involves dealing with emotions.

- Our need to **contribute** is met by our contributions to our workplace in the form of the work we do.

It's exciting to learn how our professional lives have the capacity to offer us so much. Meeting these six core human needs is something we can all achieve from our professional settings if we have the proper guidance.

Knowing this, doesn't it make sense for you to invest your time and become more intentional about the way you develop your career and professional identity?

For me, personally, it made a *huge* difference.

HOW THIS BOOK WORKS

My passion lies in helping and guiding those who are committed to experiencing a truly rewarding career that fulfills all their needs. When I embarked on this journey to help others gain what I was so eager to find years ago, I was *so* excited. And that excitement carries forward through to the present each time I start working with a new client. Every person I coach is a reminder of why I **love** what I do. Every group I engage with during a speech is a group of people that I'm invested in helping, and every article, like or comment is a step forward as I fulfill my passion.

This book scratches the surface of all that I help my clients work through, but it is filled with valuable insights that I hope will spark excitement within you. It's time for you to flip your light switch on and see what's awaiting you in your career!

The content in this book is structured to be your guide for this meaningful change. It will show you the necessary steps you can take to nurture your career and allow it to blossom - when this happens, you can discover your full potential. I encourage you to take the next step by also using the free companion workbook, which is a step-by-step guide to work through the actions suggested in this book. This will allow you to reflect and take action on what you have been practicing in your career, compared to how you can create better personal practices that will open up more doors. These are doors that lead to more professional rewards, as well as personal fulfillment.

Throughout the next few chapters, you will meet Taylor

and learn about her career journey. You're encouraged to place yourself in Taylor's shoes and learn all the ways you can begin to become more effective at fulfilling your career needs.

As you read along, remember to:

- Take notes on ideas that come into your mind.

- Recognize your ability to be intentional in your every action.

- Learn about your greatest assets to help you reach great heights in your career.

- Commit to investing your time in the companion workbook.

Mostly... invest in the *Business of You*!

Ready to jump?

1 | WHAT IS THE BUSINESS OF YOU?

"Nourishing yourself in a way that helps you blossom in the direction you want to go is attainable, and you are worth the effort."
~Deborah Day~

The lens we use to view our careers through can make or break us, both personally and professionally.

Stephen R Covey rightly said,

"We must look at the lens through which we see the world, as well as the world we see, and that the lens itself shapes how we interpret the world".

How we all choose to do that may vary; however, we must be mindful of our point of view.

What kind of lens should you view your career through to get to your perfect career?

Most people in corporate settings make the mistake of choosing the lens and perspective of an employee. This is why people don't feel guilty when they walk in late to work, do personal work during working hours, or when they don't care about the impact they have on the bottom-line of the organization. This is the lens I want you to walk away from starting **today**.

So what other lens should I use, you ask?

Use the lens of a business owner.

The Business of You is the mindset of looking at your career as a business and stepping into the shoes of a business owner.

Is it better to look at our jobs through the perspective of an employee, or as an owner/employer? The answer— it is not only beneficial, but also imperative to look at your career as a business in and of itself and step into the shoes of a business owner. You can and should make decisions that benefit your Career Inc which in turn should positively impact the organization you work for.

Imagine you are a brick and mortar store owner. Would you take time during your store's operational hours to get your nails done? Would you open the store late on a regular basis? Would you blame someone else when a customer has a complaint?

No, you wouldn't, because you take complete responsibility for every aspect of the store. So, why not adopt the same mindset with your career?

Every business in existence has many facets to it that must be addressed to ensure its success. Your career does, too – it has different elements that are crucial for overall success. Understanding this and using this in everything you decide to do is important for your career development. It will offer you three things:

1. A holistic way of looking at your career.
2. The solid framework to build your career upon.
3. A means of moving yourself toward a state of career happiness.

When we think about career development we must recognize that the process has to be intentional.

Having an intentional focus on your career development is necessary in today's world. Gone are the days where you were able to get a job right out of college and then remain with that same company until the day you retire. Listen, I'm not saying that was bad for people who had and took that type of opportunity, but it's not a realistic expectation to bank your career on any longer. This was an easy model to follow in the prior decades, because it took your career development out of your hands. You grew into the positions that were offered by the company you landed in right after college. You grew at the mercy of the company. YOU (most often) did not intentionally design your career path! You took on jobs and responsibilities based on what was available and given to you.

Today, it's a little different - we have to hold the reins of our career development in our hands, not just rely solely on our employers.

◆ ◆ ◆

MEET TAYLOR

Taylor is our case study that we're going to follow throughout this book. Here's where Taylor is at right now:

- She's currently employed for the past 3 years with the same organization

- She wants to move ahead but is unsure of how to get to the next level

- She's exploring the best career options to help with goals

- She's more than a bit uncertain about career management and steps to take on a regular basis to advance

- She doesn't want to indulge in one-time activities or schemes to get the next promotion/raise/opportunity

Taylor needs to begin by acknowledging one thing, and believing it through and through - we are not designed to grow at the mercy of our employer, but by our dedication to our own paths.

When we take responsibility for our actions, ultimately everybody wins. Some benefits include:

- Employers have more engaged employees.

- Employees have greater career satisfaction.

- Opportunities for individuals to grow are constantly cultivated.

Although many things have changed from years ago, the truth is that we live in a world where opportunities abound! Taylor - and the rest of us - have the freedom to pursue any career that we want. And, we want to participate in the journey, not just feel like we are on the cattle train being corralled to the pen destined to become our career.

Check out these career statistics that I hope will inspire you to see why the Business of You is the way to go:

- Today, 51.3% of people say they are unhappy at work.[2]

- People born between 1957 and 1964 held an average of 11.7 jobs from ages 18 to 48. Remarkably, women held almost as many jobs as men despite taking more time out of their career for child-rearing activities. On average, men held 11.8 jobs and women held 11.5 jobs. 25% percent held 15 jobs or more while 12% held four jobs or less.[3]

Guess what else we all have the ability to do? Pursue several careers at one time if we so desire. If Taylor's goal is to work in a different country, Taylor can make strategic career moves that help support that goal with tangible action! We all have a great degree of control over most of the twists and turns in our career path. We cannot control things such as downsizing and reductions in the workforce, but we can control our actions and efforts to grow and advance toward what we want. It is entirely possible to structure our career paths in this manner.

The beauty of the *Business of You* framework is that it is not rigid. It helps you adapt and be flexible to make the twists and turns needed in the face of changes. It's like a mound of play dough that You have the ability to mold in any shape with your hands; it's manipulated by your actions. So, why not manipulate your actions in a strategic manner to produce your desired outcome? For people like Taylor who are beginning their career path, it allows managing and pursuing career goals to produce the desired outcomes needed by acting as the guardrails.

In The War of Art by Steven Pressfield, he penned:

"Making yourself a corporation (or just thinking

of yourself in that way) reinforces the idea of professionalism because it separates the artist-doing-the-work from the will-and-consciousness-running-the-show. No matter how much abuse is heaped on the head of the former, the latter takes it in stride and keeps on trucking. Conversely with success: You-the-writer may get a swelled head, but you-the-boss remember how to take yourself down a peg."

What really makes the Business of You framework amazing is that it puts you in the game as a true professional, not just someone who is benched on the sidelines or talking the game while not taking the steps. People who follow this framework are people who are taken seriously in their careers and in their fields. They bear the mark of a true professional, and it shows—without them having to tell anyone. Their actions and attitude speak volumes.

Are you ready to be dedicated to your craft and give it wings? Are you someone who is serious about your Career Inc.?

What really powers the Business of You **is** YOU—and your change in mindset that results from being invested in your career. It's a change of perspective that leads to better results.

With this change in perspective, you increase your ability to go forward - like a rocket ship, ready for takeoff. Additionally, you will be ready to:

- Take on the challenges that will advance your career.

- Go forward knowing that you recognize that your actions are specific and results-driven.

- Embrace a rewarding career and be a part of the small percentage of people who are actually happy with their career.

Let's do it - get ready to change your tide.

Not liking your career is a sad reality that you can either avoid, or eventually come to terms with and then try to change the course. Either way, you will likely reach a point where you want to address it...because you want *more*. That's where the Business of You kicks in!

You hear it all the time - most people look at their jobs as something that they've **rented**, not something that they **own**. They go to work and do what they have to do. The reward is a steady paycheck and a pathway of advancement that is offered to them, often times neither without their input nor on their timeline. It's all up to the employers, and that's not bad -that is what employers *do*. But to grow and advance at the pace YOU desire, to make the money YOU want to make and to work on projects that YOU want to work on, you have to OWN your career. This is the only way you can guarantee input into the decisions that make up your professional life.

Jack Canfield, author of The Success Principles writes,

"External factors do not determine how you live. YOU are in complete control of the quality of your life, by either creating or allowing the circumstances you experience. When you realize that you—and only you—create your experiences, you'll realize that you can un-create them and forge new experiences whenever you want."

Own your career advancement.

Here's what Taylor and the others who are out there figuring out the ever-shifting pathways of a career should consider. It's a **shift in perspective**, first and foremost, and I ask you all to put a healthy dose of thought into it.

Imagine you own a business... what type of owner would you be? After all, it's a reflection of you, the person, just as much as you, the enterprise. Would you care about every aspect of your business? Or would you just care about the bottom line, while not caring about everything in between?

Successful business owners care about every single aspect of their business—no exceptions.

If Taylor decides to open up a retail store that sells electronics accessories, should she worry about the signs on the front of the store? What about the return policy?

As for reputation and reviews...are those also important? They are all very different considerations, and all equally important. They are parts of the puzzle that make up the business as a whole. The small details matter, across the board. If she employs people to work in the store and notices something is awry, Taylor needs to address it. As a business owner, she should stay on top of all aspects of the business.

This mindset of a business owner is the one you need to adopt for your career. This simple mindset shift empowers you in every way and is a constant reminder that your career is within your control—at times, more than you might imagine. And, this is okay! The more you get comfortable in taking control, the easier it'll be to naturally work in ways that enhance your fullest potential. It will allow you to recognize and take advantage of:

- Unanticipated opportunities that may arise

- The ability to be in the driver's seat of your career

- Opportunities to create your own advantages

Let's think about another example with Taylor. Taylor works for an organization that is on the cusp—growing and expanding at a healthy pace - and with that comes a need for new talents to handle new roles. Taylor's peers talk about the changes they'd like to see, as well as the usual 'stuff' about making more money, having more respect, etc.

Taylor decides to talk to the manager and express interest in moving into one of the new roles. Taylor finds out:

- What the criteria is for the position

- How to be remembered for consideration

Taylor then gets to work ensuring that the appropriate attributes are in place for her to fit the role. Taylor is growing into the goal that she desires. She does it with the mindset of Owning her Career. And that is the difference that will propel her forward.

Now, consider everything Taylor has done; who do you think is going to be remembered for the next advancement opportunity? My bet is that it will be Taylor!

Taylor is not just working hard - Taylor is working smart. Everyone can manifest this type of activity in his or her lives. Consider these possible outcomes that you can manifest with some strategy, adaptability, and willingness by adopting the Business of You:

- You can be chosen for high profile projects

- You can achieve greater visibility and interaction at the C-suite level (the most important executives at corporate level—Chief; COO; CEO; CIO, etc.)

- You can be invited to top level strategy meetings

- You can find overseas opportunities that allow you to gain global experience while also experiencing wonderful life adventures

- You can be offered stretch assignments and expand upon

them based on your valued insights

- You can be eligible to receive bonuses and salary increases from your personal initiatives and investment into your career

- You can participate in networking opportunities at high levels in the industry

- You can have access to unique opportunities that are not available to others

- You can receive next level promotions and opportunities

- Others want in - you can receive offers from other organizations

The *Business of You* framework is created in a way that it capitalizes on all that you bring to the table – your strengths, weaknesses, and fullest potential.

This framework allows you to view **yourself** as the ***product*** and your **career** as the *business* that operates around the product (YOU). In the companion workbook that supports this, you will be able to tap into the specifics that help you recognize what condition 'your business' is in, and how to begin making the adjustments that will withstand the test of time. Your Career Inc, is a full-time business for as long as you either choose to have a career.

CHAPTER 1 TAKEAWAYS:

→ Be intentional with your career and professional path.

→ Act as though you are a business owner, because you actually *are* - you're the owner of the *Business of You*, managing every aspect of your Career, Inc.

→ By taking control of your career and being proactive, success will find you in the form of opportunities, networking contacts, exciting new roles, and promotions.

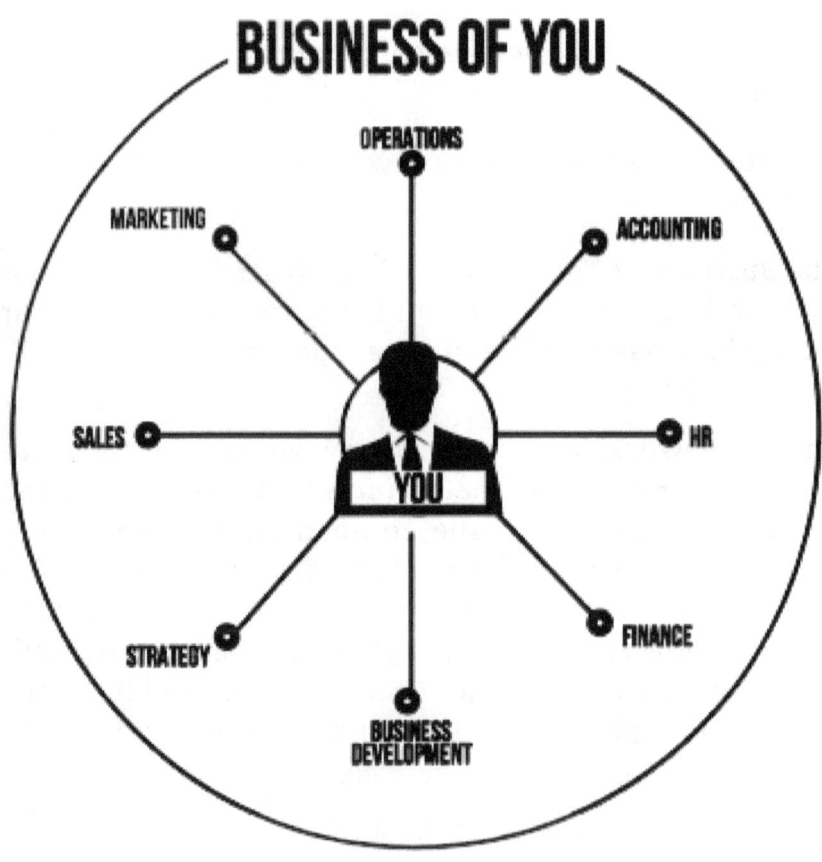

2 | YOU

"Each of us is a CEO."
~Peter Drucker~

Every business is built around a product or a service offering. With the Business of You framework, YOU are the product or service being offered.

All around you, products of all kinds in various categories are being sold, all designed to meet the needs of consumers (even if the consumers don't realize it). You may be looking at physical products that are electronic (iPhone or a laptop), food (crackers, vegetables, cupcakes, etc.), clothes, accessories, software, and so on - it's endless! Just sources like Amazon alone have millions upon millions of products that people want and/or need.

When it comes to the services arena, there are again many available, all designed to cater to individuals who may be in need of that service. These services range from simple things like lawn mowing to those services that are multi-million dollar businesses.

Regardless, if you are looking at a product or service, there is a core offering. Take Taylor's Cupcake Emporium, for example. The entire company is built around a single offering—to sell a $3.99 cupcake to as many customers as they can. In order to do this, a slew of things must take place:

- Taylor needs to procure ingredients to produce the cupcake.

- The cupcake has to be made/manufactured.

- Marketing is necessary to get the word out there that Taylor's Cupcake Emporium has "the best" cupcakes —they are worth seeking out!

- Those delicious, must-have cupcakes must sell in order to deliver satisfaction to customers, all while sustaining the operations of the business on an ongoing basis.

A business owner can't have a 'one and done' mentality, as it's an ongoing investment that takes into account the adaptability and flexibility that is necessary to meet the demands of their market (and to hopefully expand the base of who their product appeals to).

Or, if Taylor's service business, Taylor's Clicks—is going to make an impact by offering portrait and event photography services, the business needs to ensure:

- It knows how to connect with actual potential clients to

get targeted results.

- The business learns how to highlight on what makes Taylor's Clicks stand out so they can grow faster.

- The experience Taylor takes her customers through to make it memorable and unforgettable.

- Deliver high quality photographs that keep the customers coming back for more.

- Customers spread the word.

So, how do the examples given by Taylor's Cupcake Emporium or Taylor's Clicks relate to your own career development?

You are the product/service that an entire company is built around. And that company is your Career Inc. And you have to treat it right and be attentive to it at all times, not indulging in sporadic bursts of attention.

As the product for your company, what is the value YOU bring to the table?

What does it feel like when you come face-to-face with the realization that you are the face of the product or service that you've built your Career Inc. around? For me, it had a great impact and I began to look at my life and professional choices more carefully. The sense of empowerment that took over changed my life. I experienced it by taking responsibility for what I was doing and examining the results my actions produced.

> *"The fact is: You are not a manager of circumstance, you're the architect of your life's experience."*
> *~Tony Robbins~*

You are the CEO, COO, CFO, CPO, and all the other C-suite roles for your business! You can invite in mentors and coaches such as myself to help you maximize your organization, but we can only guide you in the right direction. You are the boss that makes the call in the end. Let's say it again - you are EVERYTHING.

Why look at your career. in this way? Because you must have a basic level of understanding of all these functions and how they impact your career. Yes, there are certain aspects that can be outsourced or you can seek help with, but you are the sculptor and you have to know how all these functions align together.

Michaelangelo is an excellent example.

> *"I saw the angel in the marble and carved until I set him free."*
>
> *~ Michelangelo*

He saw part of his job as the head of Michelangelo, Inc. to take responsibility for bringing out the stone's fullest potential that he was capable of doing. He wouldn't release a sculpture to the world that didn't have his personal best efforts. We shouldn't release what is not symbolic of our excellence if we didn't give it a solid effort, either.

Our purpose is to recognize our potential and use it to full capacity to make our own lives and the lives of people around us better.

By now, I hope I've delivered a message for you to digest and picture. You are the center of the framework of your organization. Without you being a solid foundation for your Career, Inc. to grow and expand upon, you are going to struggle.

A question of discovery should be guiding you right now. How can you leverage all of the functions necessary as a business owner to have a more holistic approach to your career development? If you can't find a definitive answer at this moment, don't worry. The companion book will help you, and you are always welcome to find out what types of coaching programs will help you graduate magna cum laude with a PhD in the *Business of You*.

CHAPTER 2 TAKEAWAYS:

→ Every business has a product or service to offer; in your Career, Inc., YOU are the product.

→ As the product for your company, you have to discover and decide what the value you bring to the table is.

→ Your purpose is to recognize your potential to make your life - as well as others - better.

3 | STRATEGY

"The essence of strategy is choosing what not to do."
~Michael Porter~

Your career strategy involves planning and directing the pathway to move towards your perfect career. In fact, the entire framework involving your Career, Inc. and the *Business of You* is a strategic plan. This book and the companion workbook are both the planning guides to help you move the needle on your career management and progression.

The strategies that we determine to be of value in our work lives should be detailed and insightful, while not so rigid that we force them into place. This will help us to adapt and be flexible in getting to our goal. A basic strategic framework involves:

- Identification of long term and short term goals

- Motivation for the goals — without the right motivation our efforts often fall short

- Plan to reach those goals

STRATEGY VS GOAL

"In strategy it is important to see distant things as if they were close and to take a distanced view of close things."

~Miyamoto Musashi, legendary Japanese swordsman~

What does this mean, exactly? You can have a strategy but you must make sure you treat it differently than a goal, because they are not the same. A person can choose anything to be a goal, but this is not synonymous with the definition or function of an effective strategy.

Strategy in the business world is tied to all that matters to an organization's growth, which includes:

- Expansion

- Employee engagement

- Development

- Product enhancements

- Profitability

- Reputability

- Expertise, and many more aspects

It speaks to any and all things that impact an organization's bottom line. It helps answer the question, "What do we do next? Or, what are the next areas of focus for us to get us to our goals?"

If a Goal is our destination, Strategy is the path we take to get to it.

An organization's success depends on the strategies they set in action.

Similarly, the strategy we define and use to get to our career goals will set the stage for our success or failure. The strategic plan determines the actions we take. Every action we take matters and has the potential to impact our progress towards our career goals. Hence, the importance of setting the right strategy!

WHAT IF I DON'T HAVE A GOAL OR DON'T KNOW WHAT MY GOAL SHOULD BE?

Maybe you are wondering, "I have no clue as to what I want in my career, therefore I don't have any goals. How can I develop a career strategy?"

First, know that you're not alone. I've felt this way and so many people have, too. It's normal. What you need to do is take the next steps to work through it.

In such a situation, your *goal* is to find out what you want in your career. Your *strategy* involves the steps you can employ to move towards that goal. Attaining clarity is a goal in itself!

EXECUTING STRATEGIC PLANS

Executing a strategic plan is crucial to the success of an organization; after all, it helps the organization stay focused on:

- The right set of priorities

- Identifying the right next steps

- Making decisions based on a strategic plan

There is no efficient or effective way to focus on the tasks mentioned if you don't have a strategy. Your result will be indecisiveness or you could possibly even be making the wrong decisions. Worse yet, you put yourself at risk of diverting your attention to the wrong next steps, which leads to what every business loathes and longs to avoid: constant firefighting, allocating resources improperly, operating from a reactive mode instead of a proactive mode, and the biggie—negatively impacting the bottom line!

For someone like Taylor, their energy should be spent

implementing strategies that become rungs on the ladder to their career advancement. Being stuck in neutral —or worse, in reverse—just doesn't work in the long run. If Taylor is unhappy with the nature of her work and struggles with talking to her boss about it, that will lead to burnout, depression, and disengagement; none of which is conducive to her personal and professional well-being. Taylor needs to begin to tap into the strategies that help create a better understanding of the 'why' of that situation, and revise her strategy accordingly to get her out of the situation she is in. This is being proactive and putting out the fire permanently, not just having it smolder until the next time a problem arises.

Lastly, if you're in the position where things are not moving for you, take a moment and pause. Look in the mirror - what do you see? Are you really taking responsibility for what's happening? Think about what is effective about what you're doing, and why is it the best way for your business? What strategies can you use to relay them? These are the questions that will help you develop a career in which you are an asset that helps to deliver the right results...you know, the kind that isn't red or with a negative in front of the number!

WHY DOES CAREER DEVELOPMENT NEED TO HAVE A STRATEGY?

"Choose your path or others may choose it for you."

~Julienne Connor~

Taylor is at the crux of trying to decide whether to jump

ship or to stay put and look for ways to grow in her current role. She has a couple years of experience and is still fond of her job. However, she is also curious about the landscape out there and wonders if she is missing out. With a lack of information and insight, Taylor is struggling to see which road may actually lead to fulfillment.

Here's my recommendation for Taylor. First, she's not alone, because so many people are in a similar position. Some may be in their early twenties and others find themselves in this predicament when they're in their mid-fifties. It can happen to anyone at any time.

Without knowing where to go, it is difficult to find a path to get there. Career strategy is the guiding light that will help to illuminate the path forward. Poetically stated, career strategy is the beacon of light from afar, shining out from a lighthouse on the horizon. That bright sliver of light helps your ship stay on track and move toward safety with its guidance, despite turbulent waves of the corporate ocean threatening to throw you overboard.

Without a strategic plan, you are like a ship bobbing in the ocean in the middle of the night with no concept of which direction you are heading. You control nothing, and as a result, you are letting the ocean tides and waves take you in any direction that they please. While that is not necessarily bad, it may not be what you want and not be reflective of what you are truly capable of.

Sure, you can still have a job that takes care of your financial needs without planning strategically for your career, but you will likely not advance in the manner and pace in which you want to.

Allowing the reins of control over your career to be placed in the hands of people around you is rarely going to lead to serving in your best interests and you may never reach your full potential by doing so.

Strategy forces you to keep hold of the reins; having a strategy helps you to understand what you want from your career. You're the keeper of the lighthouse and that beacon is always on for you, taking you into the future. You may not always see every detail around you, but you'll know that you are headed in a pretty great direction. A strategy is not set in stone - it can and *must* be tweaked to get to the destination. It gives you the opportunity to gauge and adjust your results as they come. If Taylor's vessel is a sailboat and the winds start blowing from the east, there's a way to adjust the mast to even that out to properly leverage the wind.

Again, as with most everything in life, nothing is set in stone. Even if you've handed the reins over to someone else for a good long while, please know that you can always take them back when you want—at will. You've got this! I am not exaggerating when I share with you that helping people take their reins back and become the head captain of their vessel is something I am very passionate about. I talk about it, mentor about it, coach about it, teach about it, and now write about it, too! I live it every day.

Don't let the reins of your career destiny be held in someone else's hands...hold on to them with a commanding grip and begin steering yourself in the direction you want to head toward.

DEVELOP YOUR CAREER STRATEGY

A typical business strategy is an all-encompassing document. It doesn't just focus on a singular objective, but the overall. It puts the meaning behind everything that you do. For most business, this includes:

- Executive summary

- Elevator pitch

- Vision statement

- Company mission statement

- SWOT (strengths, weaknesses, opportunities, threats)

- Goals

- KPIs

- Target customers

- Industry analysis

- Competitive analysis and advantage

- Marketing plans

- Team insights

- Operations plan

- Financial projections

In this book, we'll spend some time addressing all the components of the *Business of You*. For right now, let's focus on two specific to strategy:

- Vision statement

- Company mission statement

Every organization poised for growth has its vision and mission identified. Your Career, Inc. is at the threshold of growth, as well. By starting with your aspirations and your purpose you'll be able to define the strategies that matter.

VISION STATEMENT

The vision you have for your career is important. This is one of the first areas that I ask people to address when I work with them; beginning with a strong and compelling vision, everything else becomes much easier and more logical.

Start by asking: where do you see your career going in the next three years? The reason that it's a three-year time frame is that **most people greatly overestimate what can be done in one year and underestimate what can be done in three years**!

With the three-year time frame in mind, if I asked Taylor this important question regarding a career, it's possible that the answer would not be clear. Perhaps there is:

- Confusion or a lack of clarity

- No particular direction in mind

- Uncertainty about what comes next

These are very real fears and scenarios for many people. For Taylor, it's an opportunity to still create a vision statement that will help. If a lack of clarity is the largest obstacle, the vision statement can be focused on gaining clarity.

Vision statements are forward-looking statements.

A vision statement will encompass your dreams and goals for your career for the next three years.

When Taylor crafts the vision statement, it is going to have the following characteristics:

- Not be a complicated paragraph filled with technology and business jargon

- Will be a precise, simple-to-follow reminder of what Taylor's career vision is

- It will serve as a reminder of what the person is working toward

For Taylor, it may look like this:

I intend to gain insight into my career path and find the strategies that will help me move upward as I grow and learn in my organization.

For Taylor, this is a reminder of why it is important to gain clarity and the benefits that come with it.

Other powerful personal vision statements may look like this:

Through my leadership I am going to help my organization transform and improve so it is a more vibrant, profitable workplace for everyone.

I am going to connect with as many people as possible and empower them to achieve both personal and career happiness.

The steps I take in my career are going to help advance the research and information that will help to eradicate Juvenile

Diabetes.

The technical support service that I offer will help customers meet their needs and improve their business.

As you can see, vision statements can be very powerful and give you a precise reason to remain motivated and connected to your career development goals.

What vision do you have? It's time to reveal it and use it to help you create the strategy that will lead to seeing it come to fruition.

Craft your vision statement in the free companion workbook from the website.

PERSONAL MISSION STATEMENT

A mission statement for the *Business of You* is tougher to produce than a vision statement is (for most people, at least). A simple guideline to help clarify the mission statement is to remember that its purpose is to identify why a certain entity exists—in this case it's your Career, Inc.

The purpose of a business's existence is captured in the mission statement.

Let's tie this idea back to your career. What is the purpose of having a career? The easy answer sounds something like this: "It's a way to pay the bills." True, but I urge you to dig a little deeper. Superficial reasons for a career are not motivating or forward-moving reasons. You're in control of your career development now, not the company you work for. You can determine your success and outcome, and discover rewards that far surpass just 'paying the bills.'

The way to begin to go deeper into your thoughts for creating a personal mission statement for your Career, Inc. may include:

- Reflection of your intentions and actions. When you are establishing your strategy for career development it's never about 'you versus them,' it's about you finding the best ways to create the career you've envisioned.

- Journaling to tap into what your thoughts are really guiding you toward. This is the ideal time to learn about negative thoughts you have that may hinder you, as well as the hints that your subconscious mind often gives you about what you truly do resonate with in your professional life.

- Personal introspection to determine where you've fallen short in the past and why, as well as areas where you didn't take responsibility for your outcome. We all learn from our mistakes if we are not fearful of embracing them!

In order to be a strong asset to a corporation or even a business that you own and operate, you must know who you are and what it takes to be an effective leader of people. And, leadership is an intricate part of career development, because on some level—whether by words or actions, and hopefully both—you will lead yourself and others as your career advances.

For someone like Taylor, a person just beginning to understand and operate from the *Business of You* mindset, the mission statement could look something like:

To be dedicated to mastering the skills that will make me an asset to my organization.

Mission statements are powerful reminders of what someone stands for. When someone else looks at it they should think, *"yeah, I can totally see that."* You are a living, breathing example of your personal mission statement.

Here are a few personal mission statements that I found which are particularly inspiring examples. They come from people who've entered into the C-Suite and built some of the most reputable companies in the world. All attribute a big part of their successes to their focus on their personal mission statements and how they add value to their careers, as well as their organizations.[4]

Denise Morrison, CEO of Campbell Soup Company

"To serve as a leader, live a balanced life, and apply ethical principles to make a significant difference."

Joel Manby, CEO of Herschend Family Entertainment

"I define personal success as being consistent to my

own personal mission statement: to love God and love others."

Sir Richard Branson, founder of The Virgin Group

"To have fun in [my] journey through life and learn from [my] mistakes."

Amanda Steinberg, founder of DailyWorth.com

"To use my gifts of intelligence, charisma, and serial optimism to cultivate the self-worth and net-worth of women around the world."

When you look at how these individuals define their role in their success, you find a variety of personality traits and desires coming out. What you also find is a group of individuals who strategized and took the time to invest in the business of their success.

NON-NEGOTIABLES

An important consideration as you start crafting your career strategy - as well as your vision and mission statements - is the concept of non-negotiables. It is one thing to identify the ideal vision for your career (dream career), but the second part to that activity involves identifying the minimum acceptable version of that ideal career as well. In addition, I recommend identifying *your* non-negotiables. These are the elements that you are not willing to negotiate no matter the circumstance. These are elements that must be present and only you can determine to what degree they must be present in your career. They can be as simple as *"I need to leave work at a certain time"* or *"I need to make X amount of dollars and will not work for a dollar less."* Maybe you want to be able to drop your child off to school in the morning or work from home one day a week. This list of non-negotiables allows you to identify your minimum acceptable version of your career and the elements that you feel strongly about. It becomes the boundary that you draw around your professional setup.

I urge you to take this concept beyond your professional life to all aspects of your life. Identify the non-negotiables in your personal relationships, your finances, your spiritual life, your physical and mental health, and so on.

The companion workbook will take you through an exercise to identify and craft your ideal and minimum acceptable version of your career along with your negotiables.

WHEN YOUR STRATEGY GETS DERAILED AND DETOURED

Everything sounds perfect, but what happens when curve balls come your way? Well, the best option is the one that creates <u>more</u> options. Having a strategy in place will help you get to a certain place in your career, but there can - and usually will be - hiccups along the way. Remember, nothing is etched in stone. Despite our best efforts, we cannot always control - and may have to re-evaluate - many things on our strategy, including our:

- Timing

- Path

- Mechanisms

If you see the latest curve ball as an inconvenience or a downright negative experience, consider shifting your perspective. Maybe, just maybe, something better may come along for you—a better option—and when it does, recognize it and don't hesitate to go for it! We need new and exciting experiences in life just as much as we need stability and structure; yes, even - if not especially - in our professional pursuits. That is why growth is listed as a basic human need in our list from Chapter 1.

A situation like this happened to one of my clients, Susan. When she had first started working with me, she was looking to move out of a corporate career in Accounting. What she *really* wanted to do was find a role in project management. Her interest in doing something creative was high, and that was an ideal position that may incorporate her skills and her desire for creativity, too.

Admittedly, Susan had many passions and a skill set that was impressive, so it was no surprise that something happened as she was taking her path to transition into a PM job. An unexpected opportunity arose; her friend was opening a promotional products store and approached her to be a business partner. After carefully reviewing the opportunity, she happily realized it met all her needs from a career perspective; she would get to:

- Exercise her creative muscle

- Meet people

- Use her finance and accounting skills

- Tap into her planning skills

- Grow a business

Susan took the opportunity and it didn't disappoint - she loves the work! It's not about just paying the bills for Susan; it's about personal growth and fulfillment achieved, in part, through her professional life.

When something unexpectedly shows up that meets all the top needs from your career, take it!

CHAPTER 3 TAKEAWAYS:

→ Your career strategy involves planning and directing the pathway to move towards your perfect career. The entire framework involving your Career, Inc. and the *Business of You* is a strategic plan.

→ If a goal is your destination, strategy is the path you take to get to it; an organization's success depends on the strategies put into action.

→ Don't let the reins of your career destiny be held in someone else's hands...hold on to them with a commanding grip and begin steering yourself in the direction you want to head toward.

→ Every organization poised for growth has its vision and mission identified.

→ The vision you have for your career is important. With a strong and compelling vision, everything else becomes much easier and more logical.

→ A vision statement will encompass your dreams and goals for your career for the next three years.

→ The purpose of a business's existence is captured in the mission statement; they are powerful reminders of what someone stands for.

→ Be prepared for curveballs and try to set yourself up for success by having multiple options to turn to should that happen.

"All of us need to understand the importance of branding. We are CEOs of our own companies: Me, Inc. To be in business today, our most important job is to be head marketer for the brand called You."

~Tom Peters~

This may be the MOST important aspect of your career growth and progression. Again, let's tie it back to running a business. You may build the most amazing product or service, but if it does not reach the right customer, it may collect cobwebs and never see the light of day.

"Building it won't make them come!"

Similarly, you may do everything possible to develop your competencies, but if it does not reach the right people or is not applied to the right environment, you are not going to see the kind of growth that you want to see.

Steve Jobs said: "*A lot of times people don't know what they want until you show it to them.*" No one can argue that he definitely showed the world that we were craving I-products' and Mac computers. As of 2012[5], there were over fifty-five-million US homes that had at least one Apple product in them. That is half of all homes in the US! Today in a family of four, the total number of Apple products easily exceeds 8 between iPhones, iPads, laptops, and desktop computer monitors.

For those of us who don't plan on being the next Apple, how do we get people to realize they need us?

It all comes down to marketing.

Let's first take a look at traditional aspects of marketing that are applied to products and services. From a base understanding of this we'll be able to tie back to our careers. This is where things get interesting!

Marketing refers to the activities that take place leading to the sale of a product/service.

Without getting into the nitty-gritty of it, at its core, marketing involves activities that take the right product/service and find ways to get it in front of the right customers for that product. **Moving forward, I will refer to product/service as product, just for the sake of brevity.*

Through marketing, the right products look more attractive and appealing to the right customer groups and a demand for the product is created. What has taken place in that process? It is about bridging the gap that exists between the product and the customer.

There are various marketing frameworks by marketing gurus that you may have come across - 4P's(Product, Price, Promotion,Place) and 7P's(4P's + People, Processes, Physical Evidence) for example. Regardless of the framework, there are certain core concepts and activities that are relevant for all marketing efforts.

1. Market Research - to understand the needs of the market and the trends of the industry

Research plays an important role in marketing activities. Understanding the customer, the customer's needs, the competitors, the landscape, the economy are the most likely factors that may influence and shape the product. Additionally, the impact of the product reaching the customer is studied in this aspect of marketing.

2. Branding and Positioning - your product/service in an appealing manner to the right target audience

All the ads on TV that we see that make us feel like we need a product, even one we've never considered before, is a result of (and the grand scheme behind) marketing. The impressions we perceive about companies and products are designed specifically to make us feel that way. If we associate user-friendly products to Apple, it is not only because the product is truly user-friendly, but also because that is the marketing message that has been fed to us.

3. Promotion - dealing with aspects related to advertising and selling your product.

Understanding how customers respond to various promotional aspects is addressed in promotion. Some customers can 'fall' for an ad just based on what they see on the TV. Others respond better to print ads. Some like direct calls, mailers, radio, brochures, word of mouth referrals, social media ads, websites, etc. There are so many ways to market to customers today - it is leveraging the right channels to reach the right customers that is important for a company to identify.

Now let's look at how this translates to the *Business of You* framework. The success of a huge company like Apple is due to several factors, including:

- The quality of its products

- Their marketing

By identifying and educating the right customers about the needs for their products, Apple is able to paint a picture of the value it can deliver and the difference it can make in their lives. And you? You need to become the Apple product to the right audience (within your current corporate environment or through marketing to the right environment for your services).

The same applies to the cupcake store down the street. Remember Taylor's Cupcake Emporium? Just making awesome cupcakes will not suffice - no matter how delicious they might be. Taylor has to actually bring people in the door to taste the awesomeness of the cupcakes and get them to spread the word. And what better way to have people want you to succeed then for them to know you, know what you're about, and to understand why you are helping them?

The same philosophy applies to you. You have a ton of value to offer to the world, but if the right people are not aware of all that you have to offer, you will remain the best-kept secret in your profession.

Your marketing efforts need to be focused on becoming known for all that you have to offer! In identifying the right people who can benefit from all that you have to offer, the returns for these efforts are rewarding and include achieving what you desire from your career—growth, compensation, and fulfillment!

1. Address your personal/professional branding

This involves being clear on who you are as a 'product' and what you bring to the table. It's what you put forth and what you let the world perceive of you. Fortunately, we have the power to define and create our brand, as well as to create the impression of ourselves that we want. The main thing to keep in mind is authenticity. The foundational element of branding is being your authentic self. You cannot create a brand that is truly not you. If you are not a bold person, trying to create an impression of boldness may be seen as a sham. People can see through those who are not authentic and true to their image.

As Tim Ferriss stated:

"Personal branding is about managing your name — even if you don't own a business — in a world of misinformation, disinformation, and semi-permanent Google records. Going on a date? Chances are that your "blind" date has Googled your name. Going to a job interview? Ditto."

2. Do market research to understand the needs of the market/industry

If you work in the food industry it's easy to keep dishing out the same traditional dishes and have a steady stream of customers. But if you want more...well then, you want to make it to the next level so you stand out from your competition in the market. To do this, you need to tune into the needs of the customer. Begin to understand how changing the menu might impact the customer. Offer a traditional dish with a different take. Get feedback from those who are already loyal to your product.

This example can also transcend to a developer in the fast-paced, ever changing IT world. You can keep programming in JAVA like people have done for decades. You've mastered it, but what else is out there? Maybe there is a new technology that integrates with JAVA.

Using that in tandem with JAVA may be important for your clients. Is there something new that your potential client base is seeking out? You need to know these things and that requires constantly scanning and assessing the market.

In the companion workbook, there's a section that will help you work with researching and understanding the trends that relate to your career advancement. It offers valuable insight to help you begin to align with the right information to strategize your goals.

3. Promote the product or service of you to the right customers.

You are the product; the potential employer is the customer. For example, going back to the restaurant example—serving trendy fusion cuisine in a southern area may not work well in the long run depending on the demographics of people living and being attracted to the area. If you opened a new restaurant and did not send mailers to people living in the area or offer coupons to entice them to come and try it out, you might be disappointed that they didn't take the initiative to find out what you were about. You've got to let them know! Get the idea?

More than anything, you don't want this:

Don't be the best kept secret in your area of expertise.

Always be mindful of opportunities to market yourself and get in front of the right people who will value you. If you're at an event and have a chance to meet the CEO of a company you're scoping out, take that initiative. It's not about going into an instant sales pitch about you, but introducing yourself and making an impression that is favorable. Social skills are very important in marketing your Career, Inc., because our interactions with others impact a great deal, even if we are not involved directly in sales or a position that's the face of the company.

Know who you are and what you bring to the table, brand and position yourself appropriately, and promote yourself to the right audience. Applying these core-marketing principles is a key component of ongoing career management.

CHAPTER 4 TAKEAWAYS:

→ Branding and marketing your business may be one of the most important aspects of your career growth and progression. If your product or service doesn't reach the right people, you will not see results.

→ Be clear on who you are as a 'product.'

→ Do market research to understand the needs of the market/industry.

→ Promote the product or service of you to the right

customers.

→ Make sure you aren't the best kept secret in your select area of expertise!

5 | SALES

Sales is the act of converting a prospective customer to a paying customer; being successful in sales is both an art and a science. Thousands and thousands of books and trainers talk about this important facet of business all the time, starting with the psychology of selling and the tools that are needed to do so effectively.

The same applies to you, and it's true what they say about people buying from people they like. Let's bring it back to your Career, Inc. What are *you* selling? The easy answer (and correct answer) is—YOU!

You = the skills, expertise, and value you bring to the table.

Imagine a car salesman at a car dealership with a prospective customer. He knows that he has to make a sale on the spot; in order to do so, he will use every possible strategy and tactic under the sun to make a sale. The salesman has to understand why the customer is looking to buy a car, the customer's budget, and any other facet that will possibly influence the sale.

Let's approach sales from that same perspective when it comes to our careers—that first moment you have a prospect in front of you.

In today's corporate environment, it does feel like we have to sell ourselves constantly. We are selling ourselves to our peers, to our managers, to people we meet at networking events and other professional situations. Although the setting is different when compared to a traditional interview, the concepts still hold good.

For most corporate professionals, this is the moment when they are in front of the hiring manager—the one who can make an offer. What should you do when you are in front of someone who could recruit you or give you the job? There's only one thing to do—start selling. This most often happens in the interview setting. Therefore, an important tool to have in your toolkit is the art of interviewing.

Interviews are an opportunity to assess mutual fit and convey what you can do for a team and an organization. Every word spoken in an interview is geared toward the ultimate question, from the interviewer's perspective: **what can you do for me?** You'd best be able to answer, because this is your opportunity to have a potential customer's full attention. You are basically 'selling' your value to the interviewer and letting them know what you can do for his/her organization.

Let's take a step back and see what other tools are required for 'sales' in the real world. A sales toolkit typically has the following components (at the very least):

- Sales letters

- Informational brochures

- Services and product sales sheets

- Client testimonials

- And other effective sales resources and strategies that may be specific to the business you are in

How do these things translate to the Business of You world? What tools would you need in *your* sales toolkit to sell YOU?

A form of a sales letter and informational brochure can loosely translate into a resume in the YOU world. Resumes are a must-have in today's business world, even if you are referred to those ideal positions through word-of-mouth. You just never know when someone will want a resume, so keeping a polished, current resume on file is a smart strategic move.

A resume is that 1 or 2 page document that presents you and your skills and your experience to anyone willing to take a look at it. **The key purpose of a resume is to elicit interest in your offering**. Your resume should garner interest from the reader and make them want to know more. It is designed to get you to the next stage in the process.

The key to a good resume lies in presenting information in a manner that is appealing to the reader, both from the perspective of what is relevant and what matters to them specifically.

Your resume should answer the foremost question on their mind, *"What can this person do to alleviate my problem?"*

The hiring manager looking to bring someone to his or her team has a need, a pain, or a problem that they hope you can solve. By directly presenting your information in a manner that can speak to that need, you create a win-win situation.

Your resume is not about using a lot of paper to make yourself stand out, but to highlight your experiences in a way that opens opportunities. The companion workbook offers some tips and strategies to tweak your resume and make it stand out. Leverage it to build your sales tool kit. After all, we are on a journey to make your Career, Inc. an elite business that is both authentic and distinct.

Another important tool in your sales toolkit is your LinkedIn profile. Originally, LinkedIn started off as a place where you put your resume online for recruiters to look at without your boss knowing about it, but those days are gone and it is a useful tool in your social media arsenal. LinkedIn has transformed itself into a one-stop shop for all your professional needs. Take a few minutes to think about how you fit into this platform and how you can leverage it to your advantage.

Your professional summary and your expertise must be showcased on LinkedIn. Apart from playing a role in helping you find jobs, transition careers, etc., LinkedIn is a great place to showcase your thought leadership. By publishing and sharing updates about your area of expertise or your industry, you begin building a brand. You'll also find that it's a great online platform to network on. You can:

- Participate in forums

- Create conversations based on your contributions for content

- Endorse others and find them endorsing you back

- Have professional referrals from other professionals easily noted and viewed

LinkedIn is revolutionizing the professional world with its products and service offerings. You can leverage it to proactively build your network (but do so authentically!) or you can react to the inquiries and interest your profile may garner. It's a platform where people put their name at stake when they vouch for your skills or write you a recommendation/testimonial for the work you've done.

These tools need to be constantly updated and kept fresh so you can showcase the relevancy of your skillset to the current market needs.

Always remember that you are a salesman. You may be thinking, *"but I'm not a sales professional, I'm an IT Manager or I'm a <fill in your role>."* Remember, irrespective of the titles and roles you have had in your job(s), you are selling your skills and expertise on platforms such as LinkedIn and in your workplace.

Look, others may sing your praises, but in the end, it's *what* you do to show those praises are earned that will help drive your career development in a strong, forward-moving direction.

If you're a bit confused about wondering what a great LinkedIn profile looks like, you'll have the ability to learn more with the companion book, or through participating in online forums with experts in that area. For instance, check out the profile of Michaela Alexis, a LinkedIn expert who has literally built her career step-by-step just by posting on LinkedIn and sharing how she used it to land a number of coveted roles; she is now a speaker and travels the world to provide her insight on the platform. I know that my clients always have a lot of questions about LinkedIn—even those who have been on the platform practically since day one, and I would encourage you to follow in the footsteps of such LinkedIn trailblazers like Michaela.

Again, your ability to consider yourself a salesman, always, is a positive trait to have. As you master it, you'll find that you are really doing what comes naturally to you and it will begin to feel quite effortless. And, if you're worried about your sales efforts sounding over the top or braggadocious, please don't be, because with authenticity and honed-in skills, you will become a savvy relationship builder rather than a salesman.

CHAPTER 5 TAKEAWAYS:

→ Sales Is the act of converting a prospective customer to a buying/paying customer; being successful in sales is both an art and a science.

→ Interviews are an opportunity to assess mutual fit and convey what you can do for a team and an organization. Start selling you!

→ A form of a sales letter and informational brochure can loosely translate into a resume in the YOU world.

→ The key purpose of a resume is to elicit interest in your offering. Your resume should answer the foremost question on their mind, *"What can this person do to alleviate my problem?"*

→ Another important tool in your sales toolkit is your LinkedIn profile. Apart from playing a role in helping you find jobs, transition careers, etc., LinkedIn is a great place to showcase your thought leadership. By publishing and sharing updates about your area of expertise or your industry, you begin building a brand.

It's also a great online platform to network on.

→ Never forget that you are a salesperson in the *Business of You*. Others may sing your praises, but in the end, it's *what* you do to show those praises are earned that will help drive your career development in a strong, forward- moving direction.

6 | HUMAN RESOURCES

"Some people today are wandering generalities instead of meaningful specifics because they have failed to discover and mine the wealth of potentials in them."
~Ifeanyi Enoch Onuoha~

In a traditional organization setting, Human Resources (also known as HR), involves all aspects of people development and management. Broad aspects of HR include:

- Compensation and benefits

- Talent acquisition

- Talent management and development

- Employee retention

- Employee relations

Each of these broad buckets can further be drilled down to understand specific responsibilities. (*Don't be deceived by the briefness of the responsibilities mentioned. Each area is a world of its own! I am giving you a view from 50,000 feet here.*)

Compensation and benefits

This area of HR is responsible for determining and administering compensation and benefits that meet industry and market standards. This is the comprehensive package involved with employment because it likely includes one or more of these elements:

- Vacation and sick days

- Bonuses

- 401K

- Health benefits

- ESOP

- Tuition reimbursement

- Relocation benefits

- And, of course, base pay

Talent acquisition

This function of the Human Resource individual/department is responsible for selecting, recruiting, and onboarding suitable employees for the organization.

Talent management and development

This area involves managing employee performance and development. Tasks such as performance reviews and learning development fall under this category.

Employee retention

This is also known as 'employee engagement.'. The focus of this task involves activities such as assessing employee satisfaction and tweaking existing policies and processes to increase the satisfaction level.

Employee relations

This category involves tasks such as crafting various policies related to ethics, vacation, internet and security, dress code, and other areas that are relevant to the business's well-being. Many times, these guidelines and policies are what you will find listed out in the employee handbook. (P.S.: you should always take the initiative to read an employee handbook in its entirety—it can help you to avoid unnecessary situations, as well as present opportunities to engage in a conversation for clarity. It shows you care about the environment you're contributing to.)

Now let's look at the most critical HR function that you will want to address through the *Business of You* lens: the one that matters most to you is talent development. From that first coveted opportunity that Taylor, (our star of this book) gets, there should be a mindful appreciation of the importance of continued talent development. It doesn't matter if Taylor just completed a degree or has a wealth of experience. Talent development for oneself should be a continuous and ongoing focus.

Identifying and developing areas of competence on an ongoing basis is crucial to performance and satisfaction. As mentioned in chapter 1, we all have the innate need to grow, and learning is a key part of growing. In order to grow, we need to improve our people skills and technical skills.

Some people are quite fortunate to work in an organization that is heavily invested in learning and development. Be mindful that more often than not, you will need to be the leader of the learning and development areas of the Business of You. When you're aware of this, you can be more strategic and intentional about your career growth and advancement; you'll know what skills you need to work on.

Each job and career is going to have its own set of technical skills that need to be mastered. The list of skills needed for each role and industry are easily identifiable. Talking to people, staying relevant by reading and listening to industry news, and reading similar titled job descriptions are some easy ways to identify the technical/functional skills needed for a particular role.

Believe it or not, technical/functional skills are easier to identify and develop than ever before. With the numerous online courses, classes, simulation material, and boot camps, developing technical skills is easily possible.

It's the people and leadership skills that provide the most challenge and are commonly ignored.

What we refer to as leadership is in relation to aspects of people management and development. There is an ongoing debate if leaders are born or made. The truth is, leaders can be born AND made.

Dr. Paul Hersey defines leadership as 'working with and through others to achieve objectives.'

Ongoing leadership development involves learning to work with and through others. Emotional intelligence is one of the top skills that we all must develop irrespective of role, position, industry, geographical location, age, etc. Similarly, other people skills like negotiation, delegation, influencing and leading, categorized as soft skills are important skills to develop as well. Each of these topics can be learned for sure. However, they are so vast that they deserve a book or more to cover in-depth! The companion workbook will cover some of the basics in negotiation and provide tips and strategies to negotiate in a professional setting. It will also cover some of the other coveted leadership skills and provide resources to hone those skills.

From my professional perspective and opinion, any amount of personal touches you can have to improve and finesse your people skills is time well spent. Remember that people are constantly changing and evolving. The young person in his thirties has differences from the newcomer in his twenties. Understanding and respecting the positions of all generations makes for a stronger workforce and positions you to move along in your career goals with a larger base of support and enthusiasm from the people around you.

The companion workbook will help you identify the skills that you possess as well as take stock of those that are needed for your professional growth. Additionally, you will come up with a plan to develop and hone these skills.

CHAPTER 6 TAKEAWAYS:

→ In a traditional organization setting, Human Resources (also known as HR), involves all aspects of people development and management.

→ These aspects include:

◆ Compensation and benefits

◆ Talent acquisition

◆ Talent management and development

◆ Employee retention

◆ Employee relations

→ Ongoing leadership development involves learning to work with and through others. Emotional intelligence is one of the top skills that we all must develop irrespective of role, position, industry, geographical location, age, etc. Similarly, other people skills like negotiation, delegation, influencing and leading, categorized as soft skills are important skills to develop as well.

"Act your wage."

~Dave Ramsey~

This is the department in an organization that manages the assets and liabilities along with planning for future growth. As you know, finances and accounting are closely related; they can be viewed as two halves of the same coin. While accounting deals with the day-to-day transactions and tracking of money flow, finance takes the information provided by accounting and uses it to make long-term financing and budgeting decisions that help run the company effectively. The finance function works to ensure that money will continue flowing into the organization in the future as well.

When you study the topic of finance, you will find various more complex activities, such as:

- Capital budgets and investments

- Cash management

- Inventory management

- Financing

- Risk management

There are many more, but you get the idea. These topics may make you roll your eyes - unless you're a numbers person, of course. Then, they'll make you grow excited and ready to dive in and sort it all out!

In the world of Career, Inc. you have to pay attention to finances so you know how they affect your Business of You framework.

Let's focus on how finances impact your career growth and how you can help craft a budget and a plan that works for you as you move along your career path.

When Taylor looks at the options available as a new career is pursued, there are many things to consider. It's a smart idea to look at a few areas that you are interested in and do some research as to what the financial rewards and benefits are to each one. It is possible that...

→ One career may not pay as much at first but have higher advancement and overall income potential

→ The other career may pay higher at first but not offer as many opportunities to grow and advance in it

It's not always just the immediate future that is most important, although it is definitely a serious and legitimate consideration. That's why some thought and evaluation must be given to the different paths. Some are better than they may seem at first; others are not as great as they appear to be. Knowing ahead of time - now that's smart time spent!

*Note: online resources such as job-hunting sites and the Bureau of Labor Statistics are excellent resources to help you learn more about the career pathways you are considering taking.

In the traditional business/corporate world, the finance department works towards making decisions to maximize the business's value. It is all about how to invest and grow the money. Decisions such as investing, financing, dividend payouts, acquisitions, ESOPs, stocks, bonds, and minimizing expenses are commonly made.

Let's translate this to the Career Inc. world.

How can you maximize the money you make and the value of the money?

The three steps to follow in the Business of You world are:

1. Take stock of your assets (both tangible and intangible) - the companion workbook will guide you to do so!

"Awareness leads to clarity and in-formed decision making."

Taking stock of your assets involves understanding all the ways you bring in money, how much you bring in, and understanding if your skills are employable.

2. Know where your money goes

3. Put your monies to work

To begin with, this next section has some questions to get you thinking about your financial outlook. By putting some thought and consideration into these questions now, you'll be better prepared to make the most out of the worksheet in your workbook when you get to it. You may be surprised at what you learn.

Here's what you need to contemplate:

1. Your target goal salary

- Why this number is important to you

- What will achieving your target salary do for you?

2. The importance of your target salary

- Are there specific things that this salary will allow you to be?

- What experiences does this target salary allow you to have?

After the considerations above, you should have greater clarity about monetary compensation and why it's important to you. However, you must go further into the financial puzzle than salary alone, because benefits and other perks offered by an employer can hold great value.

Now, think about what benefits you currently receive. Some of the most common benefits that can be equated with a dollar value include:

- Health insurance

- Stock options

- 401(k) contributions

- Retirement planning

- Wellness benefits (health clubs, for example)

- Tuition reimbursement

- Free training and seminars

- Bonuses

Those benefits are all of great value, and an appealing part of why someone would consider working for a certain employer. Not everyone will be interested in all of the benefits, but as you assess what's available to you, there will be certain benefits that are more attractive to you than others.

Basically, benefits combined with your target goal salary all contribute to your personal financial bottom line. This is what you need for taking a more sound look at your budgeting and expenses.

While the insight I'm offering is not intended to be a course on personal finance, it's definitely meant to get you to start thinking about your personal finances and managing them properly. If you're not sure how it relates, think of these potential scenarios that might be squashed due to poor financial management:

- Career opportunities that require credit checks

- Not having the excess cash to invest in training that may be the one thing holding you back from your dream opportunity

- The distraction of financial stress

- The way you can dress and present yourself in your work environment

- Going out to socialize and build camaraderie with peers after work hours

- Unexpected health or family emergency that requires a large sum of money

- Layoff that requires a sum of money to see you through a few months

You can do more when you manage your money better. One of the best things about looking into your finances is that you can see how much money you really bring in and determine where you spend the most. It makes you more aware, which is always beneficial.

A simple way to get an idea is to log into your bank accounts and see how many credits you have compared to debits. Many banks also have breakdowns of the areas that you spend money (based on debit/credit card activity), which include groceries, gas, utilities, clothing, misc., etc. Credit cards also offer these types of analysis to help you gain an accurate picture. Websites such as www.personalcapital.com allow you to get a wholistic view of your entire financial portfolio and give you a networth number.

At this moment, without looking at any of that, how do you feel about your financial outlook?

How does it compare to what you define as a target salary?

And, how aware were you (are you) of how you spend and save your money?

When you dive into the workbook exercise for finances, this is what you can expect to happen: you are going to better understand the gap between where you are now in terms of monetary benefits and where you want to be. It will give you a whole new perspective as to how on-track your goal is, as well as insight as to how long it takes someone to reach that target salary, on average, that is in a similar position. Of course, the *Business of You* may not power them. It's exciting to keep this in mind!

CHAPTER 7 TAKEAWAYS:

→ The finance department in an organization manages the assets and liabilities along with planning for future growth.

→ In the world of Career, Inc. you have to pay attention to finances so you know how they affect your *Business of You* framework.

→ It's a smart idea to look at a few areas that you are interested in and do some research as to what the financial rewards and benefits are to each one. It is possible that...

◆ One career may not pay as much at first but have higher advancement and overall income potential

◆ The other career may pay higher at first but not

offer as many opportunities to grow and advance in it

→ The three steps to follow in the *Business of You* world are:

◆ Take stock of your assets (both tangible and intangible)

◆ Know where your money goes

◆ Put your monies to work

→ Identify your desired target salary and benefits that will contribute to your overall financial health and bottom line.

8 | BUSINESS
DEVELOPMENT

"Without customers, you don't have a business. You have a hobby."
~Don Peppers and Martha Rogers~

All businesses have some kind of a business development plan - formal or informal. Business development involves understanding and identifying how to grow the business with more opportunities. It most often involves building relationships to identify new channels of growth or leverage existing channels for new growth. Developing new partners, mergers and acquisitions, new territories, new sales channels, new products and services, new distribution channels, and other aspects fall under this umbrella.

Consider the example of a car dealership. We mentioned the sales folks earlier, but there are also marketing folks and business development folks. They each have a different focus.

- The sales folks at a car dealership are focused on making a sale to the customer. Their objective is to get the goods into the hands of the customer in exchange for money.

- Marketing folks are focused on attracting the right customers to come into the car dealership.

- Business development folks are focused on identifying new opportunities to increase the car dealership business. This may involve expansion into new territories, increasing inventory to cater to the demands of their marketplace, and exploring complementary products that add value to the customer.

Business development is everything when it comes to your Career, Inc. When it comes to business development within the framework of your career, it is all about prospecting and building relationships.

We're going to take a look at each of these activities separately and see how Taylor might approach business development.

Prospecting

Taylor is on a mission to identify a target market. In this case, it's the people in the industry and/or other organizations that would be beneficial for Taylor to build a relationship with.

Since Taylor is newer to this field there is some work

that needs to be done to figure out who the key figures are within the organization to prospect. This means that some research has to be done on the folks and it needs to be focused on three distinct areas, namely:

- Organizational culture

- Work environment

- Fit with services offered

For Taylor, finding out this specific information is going to help with creating a plan to connect with the people and organizations that will align with his/her specific goals, as well as give the opportunity to create more meaningful connections for career development. It's a targeted approach to prospecting, removing the chance of stumbling upon the right person. Taylor is showing a great initiative by seeking out this information. Next, it's time to focus on building a relationship.

Building relationships

Once you have the target individuals and organizations identified, the next phase involves building relationships and nurturing them. Very seldom, if ever, is a relationship solid and beneficial with just a simple introduction. The best relationships that lead to a joint purpose take time. You don't just attend one networking event and believe you've sealed the deal. But Taylor is very smart by this time, knowing that it's an ongoing commitment to grow and go where the right connections are.

Your Network Is Your Net Worth.

Through Taylor focusing on nurturing relationships, there is going to be a plethora of opportunities to grow and advance along her career path. This will include opportunities in any company that Taylor works for, as well as other companies that see what an asset Taylor is.

By Taylor not viewing networking as a way to get someone to do something for her, such as assisting her in getting her dream job or putting in a good word for her when she needs it and instead focusing on nurturing the relationship, she is ensuring that her networking is building up her net worth. Going rogue and not placing value on networking may leave you feeling like you're walking a tight rope without a safety net — and the wind's blowing right at you.

The way you look at business development shows a few things about you that you should always be mindful of. For starters, it shows that you are serious about your career. Second, it shows that you are an asset to your current employer, and therefore more appealing to a potential new employer. Lastly, it is the best way to ensure that you are in control of your career path. People within the organizations you work for, and within your network group, may sing your praises, but if you don't take the initiative to get the opportunities, that will mean little in the end.

BONUS: NETWORKING IDEAS

In the traditional world, networking may involve wining and dining, sending gifts, taking people out to lunches and events, sending tickets to games in town, and other similar activities. While a similar set of activities may be employed in the Business of You world as well, let's take it a step further and focus on activities that take each relationship to the next level.

You don't have to spend an excessive amount of money in order to get the benefits of sound relationship building in your professional world. These smart, thoughtful considerations can help you take great strides:

- Get involved with organizations and boards. This is an excellent way to meet people and prove that you are compassionate, reliable, and dedicated to more than just yourself.

- Develop good listening skills. Dale Carnegie once penned: *"You can make more friends in two months by becoming interested in other people than you can in two years by trying to get other people interested in you."*

- Always have business cards available to hand out.

- Have the LinkedIn app installed on your smartphone and connect with a new contact on the app as and when you meet them.

- Follow the social media pages of key players in organizations and the organizations themselves. Stay abreast of updates and what's happening within the culture. It's a great way to engage in conversations when the proper opportunities arise.

- Embrace the old-fashioned good manners of thank you notes—either handwritten or emails (although some emails may never go through).

- Make connections on LinkedIn, along with messages that say why you'd like to connect.

- Get creative and write articles and contribute to industry publications for your career that will get you noticed.

One of the most exciting aspects of doing business in today's world is that there are so many ways to network and communicate with people from around the globe. Take advantage of the opportunities that will really work for you, because when you align with the right ones, it's not a burden to participate. It's part of your passion and a way to highlight your involvement in matters that are important to you.

CHAPTER 8 TAKEAWAYS:

→ Business development involves understanding and identifying how to grow the business with more opportunities.

→ When it comes to business development within the framework of your career, it is all about prospecting and building relationships.

→ By focusing on nurturing relationships and network-ing, there is going to be a plethora of opportunities to grow and advance along your career path.

"Commitment means staying loyal to what you said you'd do long after the mood you said it in has left you."
~Author Unknown~

In the traditional world of business, there is a huge amount of legal work involved. There are contracts to govern relationships with external relationships such as vendors and suppliers. You can also find agreements with employees regarding intellectual property related work, non-compete clauses, leases, etc. There is so much that takes place that is tied to something legal in nature (not ethically, but as far as obligations).

In your Career Inc., there is most likely not going to be all of these types of legalities. However, there are a few legal matters that you need to consider—and take seriously. Just like most people like to consider their word binding, there are also some things that may come into play for your career that are legally binding.

The contracts you enter into

If you work as a contractor, you need to keep a tight tab on your contracts that you commit to so you can ensure they are legally correct and compliant. Even if you don't have an attorney on retainer, you should make sure that any contracts you have your signature on:

- Give you the protections that you want

- Are not putting you at legal risk in some way

- Work for the state/country that you live in

That little bit of extra time upfront can give you a lot more assurances down the road, lest something happen where you need to use that signed contract for validation of something.

The paperwork you sign to work for an organization

If you work at an organization, be aware of all the paperwork you sign. Pay particular attention to:

- **Non-compete clauses**—Many businesses will have you sign a non-compete clause that is good for anywhere from 6 months up to 24 months after you terminate employment. This clause says that you cannot reach out to your clients from that business in an attempt to enter into business with them at your new place of employment (or your own business if you took that step). If Taylor takes one job to gain experience with a plan of starting a new company a year later, this is important to know. And, necessary if the networking at that career is meant to build relationships for that next step.

- **Non-disclosure agreements**—These are important agreements that express you cannot share specific information with people outside the business you work for, as well possibly for the clients you work with. Confidentiality is key; if you are caught violating this type of agreement legal action can take place that ruins your credibility, can have serious legal consequences, and can even cost you a lot of money. If you value confidentiality, expressing the values of a non-disclosure agreement to others can actually become an asset in regards to your character.

- **Intellectual Property (IP) related matters**—There are rules prevalent today on the ownership rights of the work you do for someone else. Understand these rules so you are not taken by surprise when the organization claims ownership of your work product.

- **Technology related** – Another area that employees are unclear on is the use of technology and devices supplied by your employer. In a world where hacking is more commonplace, more often than not the breach into a company's systems is from employee error. When they have the policies and guidelines in place—signed by you—you should be respectful to what the organization needs you to do to help ensure their security, as well as your job security, too.

HAVE A PERSONAL WILL IN PLACE

Regardless of your age, you should have a will in place that talks about what happens with your assets should you pass away. There are no guarantees that monies will just go to whom you wish them to go to (including some types of corporate benefits) without you specifically stating as much. This is smart business and as your life changes and assets increase, relationship statuses change, etc. you should update that will to be inclusive of these changes, as well.

Legal matters make some people nervous and some people very analytical. How you respond to them should be in a manner that makes you understand them thoroughly as well as a thorough understanding of how contracts and your signature impact you at the present as well as potentially in the future.

CHAPTER 9 TAKEAWAYS:

→   In the traditional world of business, there is a huge amount of legal work involved.

→   In your Career Inc., there is most likely not going to be all of these types of legalities. However, there are a few legal matters that you need to consider—and take seriously, including:

◆   The contracts you enter into

◆   The paperwork you sign to work for an organization

- Non-disclosure agreements

- Intellectual Property (IP) related matters

- Technology-related

→ Additionally, be prepared and have a will in place, just in case.

"Money, like emotions, is something you must control to keep your life on the right track."
~Natasha Munson~

At businessdictionary.com, accounting is described as "a means of providing information on the resources available to a firm, the means employed to finance those resources, and the results achieved through their use." At a high level, it may involve reporting to investors or stockholders (financial accounting) or it may be internal to an organization and refer to reporting to management (managerial accounting).

As previously mentioned in the chapter on Finances, accounting helps track the daily flow of money in and out of a firm.

In terms of the Business of You, accounting is best described as:

A way of keeping track of how and where your money is spent.

When it comes to your Career Inc., the same thing needs to be done. You want to know what's going on with your activities and understanding the cost of what you do.

Let's zoom into Taylor's living room. Everything has been going great and now it's time for some evaluation of the outlook for your Career Inc.

You want to know that you are being a proper steward for your Career Inc. and making sound decisions about and with your money. Finances impact everything, including your career path development.

There are three areas that you'll want to always have a firm grasp on in the accounting department of your career success.

THE 'PROFIT' PARTS OF ACCOUNTING

Are you getting paid fairly for the skills you have and offer in your position, as well as the work you do? Through knowing the trends for your position and understanding what other companies offer, you can create a stronger case to ensure you are at the industry standard for wage. This leverage can be used at your current employer and definitely for future employment negotiations.

KEEPING TRACK OF YOUR SKILLS AND THE ASSETS YOU NEED TO DEVELOP

What skills do you have and what do you need to grow? This is the area where you keep abreast of all that is happening in your industry and your area of expertise. You know when you need to update your skills and take relevant action to improve them. You identify what classes and courses you need to take, which conferences are good to attend. You put together a plan to keep developing your assets and refer to it often, seeing what steps have been taken. It's quite rewarding to move an item in the 'development column' into the 'assets section.'

AUDIT YOUR LIFE AND CAREER CONSTANTLY

This may sound tough, but with the questions in the companion workbook, you can easily set up a strategic plan that works for evaluating your life and what's happening—at least on a monthly basis for some areas; quarterly or yearly for others. This way, there are fewer surprises and ideas are fresh in your head that can help all the time!

There are many personal accounting software tools that you can leverage to keep up with auditing your personal finances. The companion workbook mentions a few that are popular currently and can get the work done for you.

In the book, *Profit First*, author Mike Michalowicz writes about taking a different view of the traditional

'Sales - Expenses = Profit' equation for our businesses. He asks us to take a Profit first and thereby use the equation **Sales - Profit = Expenses**. The money that is left after taking the profit is what is used for operational and other expenses.

I am adopting a similar philosophy in the Career, Inc. world. First let's understand what we bring in the door tangibly and intangibly. Then, determine what we want our money for. Once we set aside our money for our core life requirements, then we have the remaining money to spend on our expenses (core and desired)! This is a core concept to understand and imbibe if we want to live within our means, have the life and lifestyle we have always wanted to have, have a healthy savings account, and lead fulfilling professional and personal lives.

When all is said and done, in order to be accountable for you, you have to be willing to commit to doing the accounting for the *Business of You*. This is one type of accounting that cannot be outsourced, because you are your best resource for it.

CHAPTER 10 TAKEAWAYS:

→   Accounting helps track the daily flow of money in and out of a firm. In terms of the *Business of You*, it's simply keeping track of how and where your money is spent.

→   Finances impact everything, including your career path development.

→ There are three areas that you'll want to always have a firm grasp on in the accounting department of your career success:

◆   The 'profits' part of accounting

◆   The running inventory of your skills and the assets
    you need to develop

◆   The consistent audit of your life and career

"**Productivity is never an accident. It is always the result of a commitment to excellence, intelligent planning, and focused effort.**"
~Paul Meyer~

For businesses, the term 'operations' refers to the way a business is run. It involves overseeing how the business operates on a day-to-day basis and tweaking the processes to maximize performance and improve efficiency. This is done with this goal in mind: to maximize output and thereby maximize revenue and profits.

There are many things to take into consideration to ensure smooth operations of any business. If there is a physical product involved, the supply chain component is a large part of the operations function. As we have seen in Taylor's Cupcake Emporium, it takes a ton of effort to get that small little cupcake out of the door. It involves purchasing the ingredients, preparing and producing the cupcake, then making the sale and continuing the operations to produce cupcakes on a regular and consistent basis. In Taylor's case, the benefits of a good operating system are obvious – hearing the 'cha ching' on the cash register equates to revenue (and hopefully profits)!

But in the Career Inc. world, the benefits you can experience from having sound operations include career development/management in a conscious and intentional manner, not a manner that leaves this growth to the whims of the people around us.

For you, learning to maximize your personal and professional output becomes an activity that is directly linked to better results in everything you do. You become more aware of your actions and how they impact the way you operate—not only in that day but also potentially in the future - leading to better operations for Career Inc.

Let's start with the routine that you begin and end your day with. Both of these are more important than you may realize, because they both impact the state-of-mind you are in when you first get up and as you lay your lead down on your pillow for the night. Your goal should always be to ensure that you, as a 'production machine,' are able to operate smoothly - without any hiccups, burn-out, or excuses as to why you didn't do something - thus ensuring you balance all aspects of your life beautifully and produce your best work.

MORNING ROUTINE

This is the set of activities you do every morning after you wake up. How you begin your day sets the tone for your day and can make a significant difference as to how you perform and act through the day. This directly correlates to the output you are able to produce.

"How we start our day determines how we create our life. Are you snoozing through your morning... snoozing through your life... and snoozing through your unlimited potential... Or are YOU committed to waking up each day with passion, purpose, and a plan so you can create the life you truly want & deserve?" ~ Hal Elrod

The workbook is going to give you some greater insight into what your current routine is, how you can enhance it, and what the greatest benefits are. To get you thinking about it, a sound morning routine will consist of:

- Waking up from a good night's sleep

- Fueling your body to take on your busy days

- Creating a positive mindset about your day—even the toughest or least appealing tasks that may be a part of it

EVENING SHUT-DOWN ROUTINE

This is the way you shut down on a daily basis. Similar to the morning routine philosophy, the way we wind down and shut down can have a huge impact on our performance the next day. In Cal Newport's book *Deep Work* he elaborates on the importance of keeping a distance from technology and work as a way to step into the zone of being able to do deep work.

Deep work stems from a sound night's sleep. Conditions such as insomnia are not norms, even if they are normal in your life. Through some self-care, you can learn to have a night time routine that helps you fall asleep fulfilled and stress free so your body and mind gets the reprieve it needs.

Seneca the Younger on *The Shortness of Life* (an essay written in 49 AD):

"The mind should not be kept continuously at the same pitch of concentration, but given amusing diversions. ...

Our minds must relax: they will rise better and keener after a rest. Just as you must not force fertile farmland, as uninterrupted productivity will soon exhaust it, so constant effort will sap our mental vigor, while a short period of rest and relaxation will restore our powers. Unremitting effort leads to a kind of mental dullness and lethargy."

When it comes to routine, it's hard not to think about younger people starting their career paths like Taylor. They have an abundance of energy and enthusiasm, are always set to have fun, and can function quite well on less sleep than most of us can as, ahem, time moves on. This means it can be hard to identify what that appeal may be to Taylor. But developing good habits doesn't have to come as a result of burn-out and stressful situations. It can just become a part of your business acumen as you go through life.

Think about these questions:

- On a typical day, how does your workday look? Is it chaotic? Is it always about putting out fires?

- Are you always in a reactionary mode?

- Do you plan and prioritize your activities every day, while having a buffer zone in place for unforeseen circumstances?

- Are you able to set the top 3 must-finish tasks everyday and accomplish them?

These are tough questions to assess and if you thought "Pfft, *I wish*" in response to any of them, then you need to take advantage of a few of these helpful tips to get you moving through your day better.

What I love about these tips is that they have always helped me as well as my coaching clients through the years. They do make a difference and are all worth considering.

POMODORO TECHNIQUE

This technique is a great way to stay focused on a task. Generally, you'll have a timer of some sort for this technique. You work for a period of 25 minutes and then take a break for 5 minutes. Then, repeat the process.

This has been proven to be highly effective for focused work. While this may not always be possible in a corporate setting, you can modify this to a suitable time interval. Some people are able to set their timer for 45 minutes and then take a break of 10 minutes. Try it and see what time interval is possible for you in your workplace. The idea is in the 25 minutes you are focused exclusively on the task at hand and do not check email or browse or attend phone calls etc. You check email in the 5-minute interval after you finish your main task. If you are unable to finish your main task in the 25 minute interval, you continue working on it in the next 25 minute cycle and so on. There are even online Pomodoro timers to help with this!

SORT YOUR TASKS LIST!

Our never-ending tasks on our task list get sorted into must-do, should-do, and want-to-do tasks.

Must-do are the tasks that must get done no matter what, such as submitting the report etc.

Should-do tasks are those that you should do at some point, such as sending out the holiday cards or calling the doctor for an appointment, etc.

Want-to-do tasks are tasks that you want to do, but there is no visible impact if you do not do them.

Putting your tasks into these buckets can help you identify the non-negotiables for the day (we covered this concept in the Strategy chapter). You are then able to design your day accordingly and work around it. For example: one of my non-negotiables is to leave work at 4 P.M. to pick up my son. It is something that could not be changed (for the most part) and my colleagues are aware of it, too. My meetings and my work are set around this non-negotiable task.

BATCHING TASKS

Research says that batching similar tasks causes a significant improvement in productivity because you can benefit from a certain frame-of-mind that you are already in. For example, if you are writing a set of related reports or doing market research on a set of related topics, it is easy to get the tasks completed when you are already in the research mode. When you switch to something completely unrelated and have to get back to the research mode, your brain has to undergo letting go of the momentum built up in the research mode phase and shift into a new mode.

Think of similar tasks in your workday that could be batched.

The way you operate in your day does matter. By being mindful of how you operate throughout the day, you can begin to take calculated and meaningful steps. This means less procrastination, less stress, less anxiety, and more productivity. This is a formula that is profitable to your bottom line for Career, Inc.!

◆ ◆ ◆

CHAPTER 11 TAKEAWAYS:

→ For businesses, the term operations refers to the way a business is run. It involves overseeing how the business operates on a day-to-day basis and tweaking the processes to maximize performance and improve efficiency. This is done with this goal in mind: to maximize output and thereby maximize revenue and profits.

→ In the Career Inc. world, the benefits you can experience from having sound operations include career development and management in a conscious and intentional manner.

→ Learning to maximize your personal and professional output becomes an activity that is directly linked to better results in everything you do.

→ The routines that you begin and end your day with are more important than you may realize. Setting up the perfect routines helps to balance all aspects of your life and produce your best work.

12 | PERSONAL BOARD OF DIRECTORS

"A lot of people have gone further than they thought they could because someone else thought they could."
~Unknown~

Most organizations have a Board of Directors (BoD). The BoD comprises of elected or appointed individuals who represent the stockholders and are involved in overseeing the governance of the organization.

The purpose of the Board is to:

- Leverage expertise and experience: Amongst board members, there are those who have done it, seen it, and know it!

- Offer unbiased viewpoints: BoD members act in the best interest of the organization and do not take sides.

- Foster valuable relationships: Most board members are sought after for the valuable industry and other relevant relationships they bring.

- Partake in strategic planning: Boards take active interest in the strategic direction of the firm and can help shape the strategy.

- Protects the interests of the stakeholders.

- Corporate governance: BoD members can be involved in corporate governance to ensure alignment to strategic direction of the firm.

If BoD's bring so much value to an organization, then we as individuals should also strive to have our own Personal Board of Directors (PBOD). After all, we are in business as well – the *Business of You* and we manag an organization as well - the Career, Inc.

Let's look at what form this can take, shall we?

Your PBOD is a group of people who you meet and consult with on a regular basis to grow Career, Inc. and to ensure it is moving in the right direction.

You may not need to meet with all of them at the same time,but knowing they are available for you to reach out to is important.

The traits of people you want on your personal board are:

1. **Connector**: This type of person knows and is willing to connect you with other people in their network. They have a large network and they enjoy introducing people to others.

2. **Resource**: This type of person is resourceful and knows about anything and everything. They are well informed, well read, and most often well connected too.

3. **Strategizer/Idea-generator**: This type of person is able to talk through different scenarios with you. They are able to facilitate long-term vision conversations with you as well as ideate on the short-term solutions.

4. **Reality Check/Tough Love:** This type of person brings you back to reality and can provide you with the tough love you need - ot get carried away with your ideas and thoughts.

5. **Cheerleader**: This person believes in you,cheers you on, and gives you that motivation and inspiration to move on and do what you need to do.

Ideally, it would be great to have one person for each of the traits above, though it is not a necessity. The same person can have multiple traits listed above. At a minimum, try to have three different people on your board.

The goal is to get different perspectives that you would not normally consider (so you don't land up jumping out of a moving train - trust me, it hurts!)

These people can comprise of people you work with currently, someone from the past, someone you aspire to be like to do what they did, someone from a different industry, different role, someone who is younger than you or older than you. These are the people you want to be able to turn to during those forks in the road situations in your career.

The companion workbook will take you through the steps necessary to build your PBOD and offers conversation helpers to ensure you get the most of these conversations!

CHAPTER 12 TAKEAWAYS:

→   Most organizations have a Board of Directors (BoD). The BoD comprises of elected or appointed individuals who represent the stockholders and are involved in overseeing the governance of the organization.

→   Your BoD is a group of people who you meet and consult with on a regular basis to grow Career, Inc. and to ensure it is moving in the right direction.

13 | CAREER, INC. IS NOW OPEN FOR BUSINESS

"Your work is going to fill a large part of your life, and the only way to be truly satisfied is to do what you believe is great work. And the only way to do great work is to love what you do."
~Steve Jobs~

It is my greatest hope that you are reading this with a greater understanding of how you can look at the *Business of You* as the greatest investment in your career path that you can take. It's so important to make sure that you recognize the power and potential you have when you put your career path into your own hands.

Why wait for others to offer you what you may want 'some day' when you can work toward what you want today?

The surface has only been scratched in this book, but

your curiosity has likely been awakened. Make sure you take it to the next level by taking advantage of the companion workbook that will give you some exercises to do that pertain to each chapter in this book. Going through that process will awaken you to your fullest potential and make you more confident that, yes, you've got this! Your career path is in your control, first and foremost.

This fresh lens to view your opportunities through is exciting and motivating. Not everyone will do this, and you'll soon be able to tell the difference between what you **choose** to do and what others choose **not** to do. While it's not a competition against others, you are giving yourself natural leadership abilities through these steps. You're developing skills that will not only make you an asset for external organizations, but the best CEO of Career, Inc. as possible.

I know you're probably saying to yourself, okay Gia, but is it always easy to master these principles?

No.

Is it always worthwhile to seek mastery of these principles?

Yes!

Between the workbook and taking advantage of courses and other resources that help lead to mastery (which you can check out at www.GiaGanesh.com and www.careerinc.co), you should think about your future in clearer, more dynamic terms.

Every action and step you take matters. And, if you want someone to help ensure you're taking the right steps forward, I'd be honored to be that person. I've been the Taylor in this book before—starting out and feeling invincible, only to find out that there was a better way. And you know what? Not all experiences have to be learned in hindsight and reflection. Some can be averted and you can be all the better for **not** having that experience.

Career development is important and I believe you can create the milestones of success in your professional life. This is truly what I wish for you, as you begin to form the most amazing enterprise you'll ever participate in—your Career Inc. Leverage the *Business of You* framework to help you intentionally craft and manage your career to work for you!

ABOUT GIA GANESH

Gia Ganesh is a Career and Employee Engagement Strategist, Coach, Speaker, and Author. Gia is most passionate about People Development and helping employees feel engaged at work.

At the time of publishing this book, Gia leads the People & Culture Office at a healthcare organization in Atlanta, GA. She is a member of the prestigious Forbes Coaches Council, an invitation-only association of the top business and career coaches.

Gia also holds two Master's Degrees, a Master's in Information Systems from Kennesaw State University and an MBA from Georgia Tech. She lives in the Atlanta, USA area with her husband and two sons. Her passion for personal development drives all aspects of her life, because she believes that all people have immense potential to do astonishing things and make a difference. Yet, most people have barely scratched the surface!

She's also crazy about chocolate and dreams of the day when she might own a chocolate factory in Switzerland —a dream she's had since she was in pigtails! Her newfound passion for Zumba classes and calligraphy, running her own business creating products and services, and her family life keeps her busy and fulfilled.

She is available for one or more of the following:

> Keynotes and breakouts

> Training workshops

> Individualized consulting/coaching

Whether you need a motivating or practical message to a large crowd or you need your employees to be engaged at work, Gia can deliver exactly what you need to help your audience transform their work habits and engagement levels through the challenges of professional life.

www.GiaGanesh.com

www.careerinc.co

www.careerikigai.com

Email: gia@giaganesh.com

Get your companion workbook here: http://
careerinc.co/book-free-gift/

---

[1] Do You Need to Feel Significant? Posted by Team Tony. https://www.tonyrobbins.com/mind-meaning/do-you-need-to-feel-significant/

[2] Job Satisfaction: 2014 Edition. The Conference Board. June 2014. https://www.conferenceboard.org/publications/publicationdetail.cfm?publicationid=2785&centerId=4

[3] The Bureau of Labor Statistics. Doyle, Alison. June 20, 2016. https://www.thebalance.com/bureau-of-labor-statistics-bls-2059767

[4] Personal Mission Statements of 5 Famous CEOS and Why You Should Write One Too. Vozza, Stephanie. February 25, 2014. https://www.fastcompany.com/3026791/dialed/personal-mission-statements-of-5-famous-ceos-and-why-you-should-write-one-too

[5] Half of US Homes own Apple Products. Gralnick, Jody. March 28, 2012. http://usatoday30.usatoday.com/tech/news/story/2012-03-28/cnbc-survey-apple-products-us-homes/53827254/1.